Accelerated Christian Training Series

Laying the FOUNDATION

BOOK 6

JESUS CHRIST, SERVANT OF GOD

Dr. Mark Hanby

 Unless otherwise identified, Scripture quotations are from the New King James Version of the Bible. Emphasis within Scripture quotations is the author's own. Please note that Destiny Image's publishing style capitalizes certain pronouns in Scripture that refer to the Father, Son, and Holy Spirit, and may differ from some Bible publishers' styles.

Take note that the name satan and related names are not capitalized. We choose not to acknowledge him, even to the point of violating grammatical rules.

Destiny Image® Publishers, Inc.
P.O. Box 310
Shippensburg, PA 17257-0310

"Speaking to the Purposes of God for This
Generation and for the Generations to Come"

ISBN 0-7684-2147-0

For Worldwide Distribution
Printed in the U.S.A.

This book and all other Destiny Image, Revival Press, MercyPlace, Fresh Bread, Destiny Image Fiction, and Treasure House books are available at Christian bookstores and distributors worldwide.

For a U.S. bookstore nearest you, call **1-800-722-6774**.
For more information on foreign distributors,
call **717-532-3040**.
Or reach us on the Internet: **www.destinyimage.com**

Contents

Introduction **5**

I. Wounded for Our Transgressions **10**
- A. What Are Transgressions?
- B. What Is Meant by "Wounded for Our Transgressions"?
- C. How Does God Forgive Our Sins?
- D. How Can We Be Sure That Our Sins Are Forgiven?

II. Bruised for Our Iniquities **25**
- A. What Is Iniquity and How Does It Differ From Sin?
- B. Where and When Did We Acquire Iniquity?
- C. What Does the Bible Mean by "Bruised for Our Iniquities"?
- D. Why Must We Be Purified From Iniquity?
- E. How Can We Be Freed From the Curse of Iniquity?
- F. How Can We Be Sure That Our Iniquity Will Be Taken Away From Our Children and Ourselves?

III. Chastised for Our Peace **41**
- A. What Does It Mean That Jesus Was Chastised for Our Peace?
- B. What Is Peace?
- C. What Is Peace With God?
- D. How Will Peace With God Affect Our Lives?

IV. Scourged for Our Healing **56**
- A. What Does "With His Stripes We Are Healed" Mean?
- B. How Did Sickness and Disease Enter the World?
- C. What Is the Curse of the Law?
- D. How Does the Death of Jesus Christ Heal Us?
- E. Why Is There Still Sickness in the World Today?
- F. How Is It Possible to Be Healed?
- G. How May We Receive Healing?
- H. What May Prevent Our Healing?
- I. Why May Healing Be Delayed?

Introduction

And you shall know the truth, and the truth shall make you free (John 8:32).

What Is Truth?

Truth Is a Person

"What is truth?" Pilate asked Jesus (Jn. 18:38). The answer to Pilate's timeless question was standing before him. Truth is not a series of facts or the sum of information. Truth is a Person: Jesus Christ. Jesus said of Himself, "I am the way, the truth, and the life" (Jn. 14:6). Truth is not only rational, it is relational. Religious theory that only teaches about God can never liberate the soul. True freedom is found in knowing Him. "And ye shall know the truth, and the truth shall make you free" (Jn. 8:32).

God has chosen to unfold His relational truth in various ways throughout the Bible and always in the form of personal relationship between Himself and men such as Adam, Noah, and Abraham. The unfolding revelation of God's relationship with man was spelled out in agreements between God and man called covenants. What better way to unfold a relational truth than in the context of relationship?

Truth Is the Result of Seeking Jesus

This relational truth is more than experience. Despite his great experience on the road to Damascus, the apostle Paul did not end his search for truth but wrote, "...that I may know *Him* and the power of His resurrection, and the fellowship of His sufferings..." (Phil. 3:10, emphasis mine). Job, wounded and in distress, cried out, "Oh that I knew where I might find *Him*..."

(Job 23:3). Jesus said, "Blessed are those who hunger and thirst for righteousness, for they shall be filled" (Mt. 5:6). Our finding the truth is the result of a hunger to know the Person of Jesus Christ. We do not seek truth and find Jesus; we seek Jesus and find the truth.

Truth Is a Highway

We may think of truth as a highway—an endless journey into the Person of God. All of us walking in the light of relationship with God are at some point in that journey. As we "seek the Lord" and "search the Scriptures," we advance. The **A**ccelerated **C**hristian **T**raining **S**eries has been created to help us move on in that journey into the Lord regardless of whether we are new believers or seasoned saints of God. There is always more truth for us regardless of our place along the road. "His ways [are] past finding out" (Rom. 11:33b).

It is important that every believer follow a course such as this. Although the believer may be exposed to a variety of good biblical preaching, there must be a systematic seeking after truth to provide a foundation upon which to grow in relationship with the Person of Jesus. Imagine agreeing to marry someone of whom you had only seen a pencil sketching. It is our intention in this course of seeking to paint a full and vital portrait of the Christ who is alive in you.

If you are a new traveler on the highway of truth, you have begun the most exciting journey of your life. Many parallels can be drawn between the new believer and a newborn child. It would be a criminal act to leave an infant out in the cold or in a house without someone to give him attention and care. It is likewise a tragedy when the Church does not nurture newborn Christians. If newborns are going to be healthy and grow to maturity, they must be carefully and loving fed with the truth of the word.

Truth Brings Maturity

The Christian life is a "growing up into Him in all things...until we come to the measure of the stature of the fullness of Christ" (see Eph. 4:13-15). It is important that we place ourselves under pastoral care if we are to "grow up." Even Jesus, who astonished the doctors and lawyers of His time, was entrusted to His parents' care. The Bible says, "Obey thse who rule over you, and be submissive: for they watch out for your souls" (Heb. 13:17). To reject the care of pastoral oversight is to reject God's plan to bring us to Himself and to leave ourselves open to error and the exit from the highway of our journey into the truth.

The ministry that God has given to the Church is five-phased with a threefold purpose. Ephesians 4:11 tells us that God has placed in the church apostles, prophets, evangelists, pastors and teachers. Their purpose is to mature, feed and motivate believers in their own calling and ministry. Only when this equipping is established in the life of the believer will they progress from spiritual newborn to spiritual childhood and on to spiritual adulthood.

In the life of every Christian there must come a point where we "put away childish things" (1 Cor. 13:11). As we become "rooted and grounded" in the basic principles of faith we are "no more children, tossed to and fro, and carried about with every wind of doctrine" (Eph. 4:14). As we grow and mature in the faith we are able to rise above our own problems and trials and reach out with power and confidence to minister the truth to the needs of those around us.

How the Accelerated Christian Training Series Works

The **A**ccelerated **C**hristian **T**raining **S**eries has been designed to meet the crucial need for intensive training in the basic doctrines of the Christian faith. These doctrines are revealed in the context of relationship between God and man. It is designed as a self-instruction course in which believers can journey at their own pace. You will find review questions at the end of each section of material you have studied that will help you to retain what you've learned.

There is an exercise called "Dig a Little Deeper; Grow a Little Closer" at the end of each major section. These reflective questions are designed to help you synthesize the truths you have been taught and then apply them in a personal way. You will be invited to journal throughout the study of this book to provide you with a record of your new understanding and growth in God. Journaling will help you to grow in your ability to hear God's voice and adjust your life and understanding to His purpose.

Following this **A.C.T.S.** course will stimulate and accelerate your spiritual understanding and bring you to a more intimate knowledge of the Truth, who is Jesus Christ. We pray that you will grow in the awareness of the Lord's presence as He guides you to Himself through the study of His Word.

Two Companions for the Road

During this time of new growth in your spiritual life there will be questions that come to mind. You will meet two companions throughout this series on the road to truth. They are Newly Newborn and Truly Taughtright. Newly will ask some of the same questions that you ask, and Truly, his mentor, will give the answers.

Introduction

Jesus Christ, Servant of God

"Behold, My Servant"...These are the words of God through the prophet Isaiah concerning Jesus Christ, the Servant of God. As we said in the previous section of teaching, Jesus emptied Himself of all power and position as God, taking the form of a servant. His purpose as the Servant of God was to bring us back into relationship with God by doing what we could not do for ourselves. A single transgression by Adam and Eve introduced a fallen nature of iniquity, which in turn resulted in the loss of peace between God and man, and ushered in the reign of sickness and death. Man was in no way able to broach the darkness that existed between himself and his Creator. Isaiah tells us prophetically what Jesus would do hundreds of years later.

> *But He was wounded for our transgressions, He was bruised for our iniquities; the chastisement for our peace was upon Him, and by His stripes we are healed* (Isaiah 53:5).

Notice that Jesus, the Servant of God, would reverse all that resulted from the Fall. He would deal with the transgression, then the perverse nature of iniquity, and then He would restore our peace and finally heal us of the result of our rebellion, which is sickness and death. In this section we will study this ministry of Jesus, the Servant of God, in greater detail. Remember the following Scripture as you walk through this chapter.

> *Just as the Son of Man did not come to be served, but to serve, and to give His life a ransom for many* (Matthew 20:28).

Let us now look at what Jesus did for us as the "Servant of God."

I. Wounded for Our Transgressions

A. What Are Transgressions?

1. Transgressions are willful and defiling acts of sin. They are stains of rebellion.

But if you do not do so, then take note, you have sinned against the Lord; and be sure your sin will find you out (Numbers 32:23).

Then He tells them their work and their transgressions—that they have acted defiantly (Job 36:9).

2. Transgressions are a "going beyond" the bounds of God's laws and ways.

All we like sheep have gone astray; we have turned, every one, to his own way; and the Lord has laid on Him the iniquity of us all (Isaiah 53:6).

They have all turned aside; they have together become unprofitable; there is none who does good, no, not one (Romans 3:12).

B. What Is Meant by "Wounded for Our Transgressions"?

1. The law of God demands the shedding of blood to forgive man's sin. This word "wounded" could also be translated "pierced," which points to Christ's death by crucifixion.

For the life of the flesh is in the blood, and I have given it to you upon the altar to make atonement for your souls; for it is the blood that makes atonement for the soul (Leviticus 17:11).

And according to the law almost all things are purified with blood, and without shedding of blood there is no remission (Hebrews 9:22).

2. Jesus became the sacrifice and shed His own blood for the forgiveness of our sins.

Much more then, having now been justified by His blood, we shall be saved from wrath through Him (Romans 5:9).

Christ has redeemed us from the curse of the law, having become a curse for us (for it is written, "Cursed is everyone who hangs on a tree") (Galatians 3:13).

In Him we have redemption through His blood, the forgiveness of sins, according to the riches of His grace (Ephesians 1:7).

3. Jesus took our place and became sin for us.

The next day John saw Jesus coming toward him, and said, "Behold! The Lamb of God who takes away the sin of the world!" (John 1:29)

For He made Him who knew no sin to be sin for us, that we might become the righteousness of God in Him (2 Corinthians 5:21).

Who Himself bore our sins in His own body on the tree, that we, having died to sins, might live for righteousness—by whose stripes you were healed (1 Peter 2:24).

C. How Does God Forgive Our Sins?

1. God forgives and forgets our sins when we confess them.

I acknowledged my sin to You, and my iniquity I have not hidden. I said, "I will confess my transgressions to the Lord," and You forgave the iniquity of my sin (Psalm 32:5).

I, even I, am He who blots out your transgressions for My own sake; and I will not remember your sins (Isaiah 43:25).

If we confess our sins, He is faithful and just to forgive us our sins and to cleanse us from all unrighteousness (1 John 1:9).

2. God forgives our sins when we turn from them. (The Bible calls this repentance.)

Repent therefore and be converted, that your sins may be blotted out, so that times of refreshing may come from the presence of the Lord (Acts 3:19).

Truly, these times of ignorance God overlooked, but now commands all men everywhere to repent (Acts 17:30).

For godly sorrow produces repentance leading to salvation, not to be regretted; but the sorrow of the world produces death (2 Corinthians 7:10).

3. God forgives our sins when we ask Him for forgiveness.

Ask, and it will be given to you; seek, and you will find; knock, and it will be opened to you (Matthew 7:7).

And whatever you ask in My name, that I will do, that the Father may be glorified in the Son. If you ask anything in My name, I will do it (John 14:13-14).

Confess your trespasses to one another, and pray for one another, that you may be healed. The effective, fervent prayer of a righteous man avails much (James 5:16).

D. How Can We Be Sure That Our Sins Are Forgiven?

1. WORD: We can be sure our sins are forgiven because the Word of God says they are forgiven when we believe on the name of Jesus Christ.

"Come now, and let us reason together," says the Lord, "Though your sins are like scarlet, they shall be as white as snow; though they are red like crimson, they shall be as wool. If you are willing and obedient, you shall eat the good of the land" (Isaiah 1:18-19).

My little children, these things I write to you, so that you may not sin. And if anyone sins, we have an Advocate with the Father, Jesus Christ the righteous (1 John 2:1).

These things I have written to you who believe in the name of the Son of God, that you may know that you have eternal life, and that you may continue to believe in the name of the Son of God (1 John 5:13).

2. WITNESS: We can be sure our sins are forgiven because of the witness of the Holy Spirit. God sends the Holy Spirit to assure us that we now belong to Him. Now we are led by the Spirit rather than our own desires.

For there are three that bear witness in heaven: the Father, the Word, and the Holy Spirit; and these three are one. And there are three that bear witness on earth: the Spirit, the water, and the blood; and these three agree as one (1 John 5:7-8).

But I said: "How can I put you among the children and give you a pleasant land, a beautiful heritage of the hosts of nations?" And I said: "You shall call Me, 'My Father,' and not turn away from Me" (Jeremiah 3:19).

For as many as are led by the Spirit of God, these are sons of God. For you did not receive the spirit of bondage again to fear, but you received the Spirit of adoption by whom we cry out, "Abba, Father." The Spirit Himself bears witness with our spirit that we are children of God (Romans 8:14-16).

And because you are sons, God has sent forth the Spirit of His Son into your hearts, crying out, "Abba, Father!" (Galatians 4:6)

3. WATER: We can be sure that our sins are forgiven as we demonstrate new faith and obedience by going through water baptism. (This is a circumcision of heart.)

Then Peter said to them, "Repent, and let every one of you be baptized in the name of Jesus Christ for the remission of sins; and you shall receive the gift of the Holy Spirit (Acts 2:38).

And now why are you waiting? Arise and be baptized, and wash away your sins, calling on the name of the Lord (Acts 22:16).

Let's Review What We Have Learned About the Servant of God.

1. The law of God demands the ________________ to forgive man's sin.

2. Jesus took our ________________ before God and became ________________ for us.

3. What three key words assure us that we are forgiven of our sins? (Hint: they all begin with W.)

____

____

____

4. *If we* ________________ *our sins, He is faithful and just to* ______________________ *us our sins and to cleanse us from all* ___________________ (1 John 1:9).

5. God forgives our sins when we ___________________ from them. (The Bible calls this repentance.)

Dig a Little Deeper; Grow a Little Closer

1. Read these verses and respond to the questions that follow.

Therefore by the deeds of the law no flesh will be justified in His sight, for by the law is the knowledge of sin. But now the righteousness of God apart from the law is revealed, being witnessed by the Law and the Prophets, even the righteousness of God, through faith in Jesus Christ, to all and on all who believe. For there is no difference; for all have sinned and fall short of the glory of God, being justified freely by His grace through the redemption that is in Christ Jesus (Romans 3:20-24).

2. According to verse 21, what can we do in our own flesh, our own efforts, to save ourselves?

____

3. According to verse 22, to whom does the righteousness of God come?

____

4. Sometimes our salvation by grace through faith in Jesus just seems too good to be true. Are there sins in your life, past or present, that you feel could not be forgiven through trusting Christ? List any that come to mind, then commit them to the

Lord and receive total forgiveness in the name of Jesus Christ. Your Father is waiting for you.

____

____

____

Review Notes

Wounded for Our Transgressions

Wounded for Our Transgressions

Wounded for Our Transgressions

II. Bruised for Our Iniquities

A. What Is Iniquity and How Does It Differ From Sin?

1. Transgressions are acts of sin while iniquity is the evil nature born in us.

Behold, I was brought forth in iniquity, and in sin my mother conceived me (Psalm 51:5).

2. Iniquity is the sinful self-serving attitude that breeds transgressions.

Among whom also we all once conducted ourselves in the lusts of our flesh, fulfilling the desires of the flesh and of the mind, and were by nature children of wrath, just as the others (Ephesians 2:3).

3. Transgressions refer to the outward acts of sin. Iniquity refers to the inward and crooked bent toward sin.

And He said, "What comes out of a man, that defiles a man. For from within, out of the heart of men, proceed evil thoughts, adulteries, fornications, murders, thefts, covetousness, wickedness, deceit, lewdness, an evil eye, blasphemy, pride, foolishness. All these evil things come from within and defile a man" (Mark 7:20-23).

B. Where and When Did We Acquire Iniquity?

1. We acquired iniquity from our forefathers.

Who can bring a clean thing out of an unclean? No one! (Job 14:4)

Behold, I was brought forth in iniquity, and in sin my mother conceived me (Psalm 51:5).

We have sinned with our fathers, we have committed iniquity, we have done wickedly (Psalm 106:6).

That which is born of the flesh is flesh, and that which is born of the Spirit is spirit (John 3:6).

Among whom also we all once conducted ourselves in the lusts of our flesh, fulfilling the desires of the flesh and of the mind, and were by nature children of wrath, just as the others (Ephesians 2:3).

2. Iniquity is referred to as "the old man" or "the body of sin."

Knowing this, that our old man was crucified with Him, that the body of sin might be done away with, that we should no longer be slaves of sin (Romans 6:6).

That you put off, concerning your former conduct, the old man which grows corrupt according to the deceitful lusts (Ephesians 4:22).

Do not lie to one another, since you have put off the old man with his deeds, and have put on the new man who is renewed in knowledge according to the image of Him who created him (Colossians 3:9-10).

C. What Does the Bible Mean by "Bruised for Our Iniquities"?

1. To be bruised is to be utterly crushed as under the weight of our iniquity.

Surely He has borne our griefs and carried our sorrows; yet we esteemed Him stricken, smitten by God, and afflicted (Isaiah 53:4).

All we like sheep have gone astray; we have turned, every one, to his own way; and the Lord has laid on Him the iniquity of us all (Isaiah 53:6).

He shall see the labor of His soul, and be satisfied. By His knowledge My righteous Servant shall justify many, for He shall bear their iniquities (Isaiah 53:11).

2. Jesus Christ was crushed for our iniquity that we might be freed from the power of the sinful nature we inherited from our forefathers.

He shall see the labor of His soul, and be satisfied. By His knowledge My righteous Servant shall justify many, for He shall bear their iniquities (Isaiah 53:11).

Therefore, just as through one man sin entered the world, and death through sin, and thus death spread to all men, because all sinned...Therefore, as through one man's offense judgment came to all men, resulting in condemnation, even so through one Man's righteous act the free gift came to all men, resulting in justification of life (Romans 5:12,18).

D. Why Must We Be Purified From Iniquity?

1. We must be freed from iniquity because God looks at our hearts.

The heart is deceitful above all things, and desperately wicked; who can know it? (Jeremiah 17:9).

Then the Lord saw that the wickedness of man was great in the earth, and that every intent of the thoughts of his heart was only evil continually (Genesis 6:5).

If I regard iniquity in my heart, the Lord will not hear (Psalm 66:18).

2. We must be purified from iniquity because our hearts are the source of sin.

For out of the heart proceed evil thoughts, murders, adulteries, fornications, thefts, false witness, blasphemies (Matthew 15:19).

3. We must be purified from iniquity to live a life that pleases God.

Because the carnal mind is enmity against God; for it is not subject to the law of God, nor indeed can be. So then, those who are in the flesh cannot please God (Romans 8:7-8).

E. How Can We Be Freed From the Curse of Iniquity?

1. We can be freed from iniquity by confessing our unrighteousness to God.

And David's heart condemned him after he had numbered the people. So David said to the Lord, "I have sinned greatly in what I have done; but now, I pray, O Lord, take away the iniquity of Your servant, for I have done very foolishly" (2 Samuel 24:10).

I acknowledged my sin to You, and my iniquity I have not hidden. I said, "I will confess my transgressions to the Lord," and You forgave the iniquity of my sin (Psalm 32:5).

2. We can be freed from iniquity by turning from sinful ways.

Yet when they come to themselves...and repent...saying, "We have sinned and done wrong, we have committed wickedness"; and when they return to You with all their heart and with all their soul...and pray to You...then hear in heaven Your dwelling place their prayer...and forgive Your people who have sinned against You, and all their transgressions which they have transgressed against You; and grant them compassion before those who took them captive, that they may have compassion on them (1 Kings 8:47-50).

O Israel, return to the Lord your God, for you have stumbled because of your iniquity; take words with you, and return to the Lord. Say to Him, "Take away all iniquity; receive us graciously, for we will offer the sacrifices of our lips" (Hosea 14:1-2).

And saying, "Repent, for the kingdom of heaven is at hand!" (Matthew 3:2)

3. We can be freed from iniquity by being baptized in water, separating us from our sinful nature, and entering into our new nature in Christ Jesus.

Jesus answered, "Most assuredly, I say to you, unless one is born of water and the Spirit, he cannot enter the kingdom of God" (John 3:5).

For as many of you as were baptized into Christ have put on Christ (Galatians 3:27).

In Him you were also circumcised with the circumcision made without hands, by putting off the body of the sins of the flesh, by the circumcision of Christ, buried with Him in baptism, in which you also were raised with Him through faith in the working of God, who raised Him from the dead (Colossians 2:11-12).

F. How Can We Be Sure That Our Iniquity Will Be Taken Away From Our Children and Ourselves?

We can be sure because God's Word tells us that Jesus has redeemed us from all iniquity.

Who is a God like You, pardoning iniquity and passing over the transgression of the remnant of His heritage? He does not retain His anger forever, because He delights in mercy. He will again have compassion on us, and will subdue our iniquities. You will cast all our sins into the depths of the sea (Micah 7:18-19).

Looking for the blessed hope and glorious appearing of our great God and Savior Jesus Christ, who gave Himself for us, that He might redeem us from every lawless deed and purify for Himself His own special people, zealous for good works (Titus 2:13-14).

> *For Christ also suffered once for sins, the just for the unjust, that He might bring us to God, being put to death in the flesh but made alive by the Spirit* (1 Peter 3:18).

Let's Review What We Have Learned About the Servant of God.

1. Transgressions are acts of sin, while iniquity is the ________________ nature born in us.

2. Jesus Christ was crushed for our ________________ that we might be freed from the power of the ________________ nature we inherited from our forefathers.

3. We acquired iniquity from our ________________.

4. Transgressions refer to the ________________ acts of sin. Iniquity refers to the ________________ and crooked bent toward sin.

5. Iniquity is referred to as the ________________ or the ________________.

6. We must be ________________ from iniquity to live a life that ________________God.

Dig a Little Deeper; Grow a Little Closer

1. Read these verses and then respond to the questions that follow.

> *Behold, I was brought forth in iniquity, and in sin my mother conceived me. Behold, You desire truth in the inward parts, and in the hidden part You will make me*

to know wisdom. Purge me with hyssop, and I shall be clean; wash me, and I shall be whiter than snow. Make me to hear joy and gladness, that the bones You have broken may rejoice. Hide Your face from my sins, and blot out all my iniquities. Create in me a clean heart, O God, and renew a steadfast spirit within me. Do not cast me away from Your presence, and do not take Your Holy Spirit from me. Restore to me the joy of Your salvation, and uphold me by Your generous Spirit (Psalm 51:5-12).

2. King David wrote this Psalm after his sins of adultery and murder were revealed to the prophet and the prophet confronted him. What did David say that the Lord desired and what did he ask the Lord to do?

____

____

____

3. Beginning in verse 10, David asked that the Lord would do six specific things for him that he could not do for himself. List those things here.

____

____

____

____

____

____

4. Are there times when you feel distant from the presence of God? Do you experience real joy in your life? Ask the Lord to reveal anything to you that He wants to wash from you. Then ask Him to do the same things that David asked.

____

____

Review Notes

Bruised for Our Iniquities

Bruised for Our Iniquities

Bruised for Our Iniquities

III. Chastised for Our Peace

A. What Does It Mean That Jesus Was Chastised for Our Peace?

1. *Chastised* means "corrected or disciplined." Men's hardened hearts could not receive the instruction of God; therefore Jesus suffered discipline for us.

O Lord, are not Your eyes on the truth? You have stricken them, but they have not grieved; You have consumed them, but they have refused to receive correction. They have made their faces harder than rock; they have refused to return (Jeremiah 5:3).

Thus says the Lord of hosts, the God of Israel: "Go and tell the men of Judah and the inhabitants of Jerusalem, 'Will you not receive instruction to obey My words?' says the Lord" (Jeremiah 35:13).

2. *Chastisement* means "direction with a rod of correction." Jesus took the blows of our instruction.

Foolishness is bound up in the heart of a child; the rod of correction will drive it far from him (Proverbs 22:15).

Who Himself bore our sins in His own body on the tree, that we, having died to sins, might live for righteousness—by whose stripes you were healed (1 Peter 2:24).

B. What Is Peace?

1. Peace is a state of wholeness, completeness, and rest.

Finally, brethren, farewell. Become complete. Be of good comfort, be of one mind, live in peace; and the God of love and peace will be with you (2 Corinthians 13:11).

2. Peace is the total absence of fear.

These things I have spoken to you, that in Me you may have peace. In the world you will have tribulation; but be of good cheer, I have overcome the world (John 16:33).

For God has not given us a spirit of fear, but of power and of love and of a sound mind (2 Timothy 1:7).

For you did not receive the spirit of bondage again to fear, but you received the Spirit of adoption by whom we cry out, "Abba, Father" (Romans 8:15).

3. Peace is a state of rest and harmony between people and God.

Moreover I will make a covenant of peace with them, and it shall be an everlasting covenant with them; I will establish them and multiply them, and I will set My sanctuary in their midst forevermore (Ezekiel 37:26).

But now in Christ Jesus you who once were far off have been brought near by the blood of Christ. For He Himself is our peace, who has made both one, and has broken down the middle wall of separation, having abolished in His flesh the enmity, that is, the law of commandments contained in ordinances, so as to create in Himself one new man from the two, thus making peace, and that He might reconcile them both to God in one body through the cross, thereby putting to death the enmity (Ephesians 2:13-16).

C. What Is Peace With God?

1. Peace with God is a restored relationship with God through Jesus Christ.

The word which God sent to the children of Israel, preaching peace through Jesus Christ—He is Lord of all (Acts 10:36).

Therefore, having been justified by faith, we have peace with God through our Lord Jesus Christ (Romans 5:1).

Now all things are of God, who has reconciled us to Himself through Jesus Christ, and has given us the ministry of reconciliation, that is, that God was in Christ reconciling the world to Himself, not imputing their trespasses to them, and has committed to us the word of reconciliation. Now then, we are ambassadors for Christ, as though God were pleading through us: we implore you on Christ's behalf, be reconciled to God (2 Corinthians 5:18-20).

And by Him to reconcile all things to Himself, by Him, whether things on earth or things in heaven, having made peace through the blood of His cross (Colossians 1:20).

Now may the God of peace who brought up our Lord Jesus from the dead, that great Shepherd of the sheep, through the blood of the everlasting covenant, make you complete in every good work to do His will, working in you what is well pleasing in His sight, through Jesus Christ, to whom be glory forever and ever. Amen (Hebrews 13:20-21).

2. Peace with God is a total dependence upon God resulting in the rest of God.

Or let him take hold of My strength, that he may make peace with Me; and he shall make peace with Me (Isaiah 27:5).

I will both lie down in peace, and sleep; for You alone, O Lord, make me dwell in safety (Psalm 4:8).

The work of righteousness will be peace, and the effect of righteousness, quietness and assurance forever. My people will dwell in a peaceful habitation, in secure dwellings, and in quiet resting places (Isaiah 32:17-18).

3. Peace is a characteristic of the Kingdom of God.

For unto us a Child is born, unto us a Son is given; and the government will be upon His shoulder. And His name will be called Wonderful, Counselor, Mighty God, Everlasting Father, Prince of Peace. Of the increase of His government and peace there will be no end, upon the throne of David and over His kingdom, to order it and establish it with judgment and justice from that time forward, even forever. The zeal of the Lord of hosts will perform this (Isaiah 9:6-7).

Yes, He shall build the temple of the Lord. He shall bear the glory, and shall sit and rule on His throne; so He shall be a priest on His throne, and the counsel of peace shall be between them both (Zechariah 6:13).

For the kingdom of God is not eating and drinking, but righteousness and peace and joy in the Holy Spirit (Romans 14:17).

4. Peace is a fruit of the Holy Spirit.

But the fruit of the Spirit is love, joy, peace, longsuffering, kindness, goodness, faithfulness, gentleness, self-control. Against such there is no law (Galatians 5:22-23).

But above all these things put on love, which is the bond of perfection. And let the peace of God rule in your hearts, to which also you were called in one body; and be thankful (Colossians 3:14-15).

Now may the Lord of peace Himself give you peace always in every way. The Lord be with you all (2 Thessalonians 3:16).

Be anxious for nothing, but in everything by prayer and supplication, with thanksgiving, let your requests be made known to God; and the peace of God, which surpasses all understanding, will guard your hearts and minds through Christ Jesus (Philippians 4:6-7).

D. How Will Peace With God Affect Our Lives?

1. Peace with God provides us with an inner quietness.

And the peace of God, which surpasses all understanding, will guard your hearts and minds through Christ Jesus (Philippians 4:7).

When He gives quietness, who then can make trouble? And when He hides His face, who then can see Him, whether it is against a nation or a man alone? (Job 34:29)

2. Peace with God provides freedom from the feelings of guilt and shame.

There is therefore now no condemnation to those who are in Christ Jesus, who do not walk according to the flesh, but according to the Spirit (Romans 8:1).

For the Scripture says, "Whoever believes on Him will not be put to shame" (Romans 10:11).

3. Peace with God gives us strength in the midst of trouble.

Yea, though I walk through the valley of the shadow of death, I will fear no evil; for You are with me; Your rod and Your staff, they comfort me. You prepare a table before me in the presence of my enemies; You anoint my head with oil; my cup runs over (Psalm 23:4-5).

Peace I leave with you, My peace I give to you; not as the world gives do I give to you. Let not your heart be troubled, neither let it be afraid (John 14:27).

These things I have spoken to you, that in Me you may have peace. In the world you will have tribulation; but be of good cheer, I have overcome the world (John 16:33).

4. Peace with God leads to peace with others in the body of Christ.

Now may the God of patience and comfort grant you to be like-minded toward one another, according to Christ Jesus, that you may with one mind and one mouth glorify the God and Father of our Lord Jesus Christ (Romans 15:5-6).

Finally, brethren, farewell. Become complete. Be of good comfort, be of one mind, live in peace; and the God of love and peace will be with you (2 Corinthians 13:11).

Let's Review What We Have Learned About the Servant of God.

1. Peace is a state of ________________, ________________, and rest.

2. Peace is a state of ________________ and ________________ between people and God.

3. Peace with God is a restored ________________ with God through ________________.

4. Peace with God provides us with an inner ______________.

5. Peace with God is a total ___________ upon God resulting in the ________________ of God.

6. Peace with God leads to ______________ with others in the ________________ of Christ.

Dig a Little Deeper; Grow a Little Closer

1. Read the verses below and respond to the questions that follow.

> *Be anxious for nothing, but in everything by prayer and supplication, with thanksgiving, let your requests be made known to God; and the peace of God, which surpasses all understanding, will guard your hearts and minds through Christ Jesus* (Philippians 4:6-7).

2. What do these verses tell us to do with things we might worry about?

____

____

____

3. What does verse 7 tell us that the peace of God surpasses? How do you think this helps us when we don't understand the circumstances we are in?

____

____

____

4. Are there things that you do not understand or have peace about right now? List those things here and then follow the instructions that these verses give us.

____

____

____

Review Notes

Chastised for Our Peace

Chastised for Our Peace

IV. Scourged for Our Healing

A. What Does "With His Stripes We Are Healed" Mean?

1. This means that the sickness and disease of a fallen world were beaten into the body of Jesus.

When evening had come, they brought to Him many who were demon-possessed. And He cast out the spirits with a word, and healed all who were sick, that it might be fulfilled which was spoken by Isaiah the prophet, saying: "He Himself took our infirmities and bore our sicknesses" (Matthew 8:16-17).

Who Himself bore our sins in His own body on the tree, that we, having died to sins, might live for righteousness—by whose stripes you were healed (1 Peter 2:24).

2. It means that we are joined with Christ in His victory over sin, sickness and death.

And these signs will follow those who believe: In My name they will cast out demons; they will speak with new tongues; they will take up serpents; and if they drink anything deadly, it will by no means hurt them; they will lay hands on the sick, and they will recover (Mark 16:17-18).

Let it be known to you all, and to all the people of Israel, that by the name of Jesus Christ of

Nazareth, whom you crucified, whom God raised from the dead, by Him this man stands here before you whole (Acts 4:10).

B. How Did Sickness and Disease Enter the World?

1. Sickness entered the world when Adam sinned against God.

But of the tree of the knowledge of good and evil you shall not eat, for in the day that you eat of it you shall surely die (Genesis 2:17).

Fools, because of their transgression, and because of their iniquities, were afflicted (Psalms 107:17).

2. Sickness entered the world when man gave dominion over to satan. Satan uses sickness and disease to destroy man, whom God loves.

So satan went out from the presence of the Lord, and struck Job with painful boils from the sole of his foot to the crown of his head (Job 2:7).

The thief does not come except to steal, and to kill, and to destroy. I have come that they may have life, and that they may have it more abundantly (John 10:10).

C. What Is the Curse of the Law?

1. The curse of the Law was the consequences of disobedience to God's Law.

But it shall come to pass, if you do not obey the voice of the Lord your God, to observe carefully all His commandments and His statutes which I command you today, that all these curses will come upon you and overtake you...The Lord will make the plague cling to you until He has consumed you from the land which you are going to possess (Deuteronomy 28:15,21).

2. The curse of the Law consists of every plague and sickness that result from disobedience to God.

The Lord will strike you with consumption, with fever, with inflammation, with severe burning fever, with the sword, with scorching, and with mildew; they shall pursue you until you perish...The Lord will strike you with the boils of Egypt, with tumors, with the scab, and with the itch, from which you cannot be healed. The Lord will strike you with madness and blindness and confusion of heart (Deuteronomy 28:22,27-28).

D. How Does the Death of Jesus Christ Heal Us?

1. Jesus took upon Himself all the curses of sin, which include sickness and disease.

For He made Him who knew no sin to be sin for us, that we might become the righteousness of God in Him (2 Corinthians 5:21).

Christ has redeemed us from the curse of the law, having become a curse for us (for it is written, "Cursed is everyone who hangs on a tree") (Galatians 3:13).

2. Jesus destroyed the power of satan over man.

Behold, I will bring it health and healing; I will heal them and reveal to them the abundance of peace and truth (Jeremiah 33:6).

And you, being dead in your trespasses and the uncircumcision of your flesh, He has made alive together with Him, having forgiven you all trespasses, having wiped out the handwriting of requirements that was against us, which was contrary to us. And He has taken it out of the way, having nailed it to the cross. Having disarmed principalities and powers, He made a public spectacle of them, triumphing over them in it (Colossians 2:13-15).

E. Why Is There Still Sickness in the World Today?

1. There is still sickness in the world because people do not realize that Jesus Christ purchased healing for all men.

My people are destroyed for lack of knowledge. Because you have rejected knowledge, I also will reject you from being priest for Me; because you have forgotten the law of your God, I also will forget your children (Hosea 4:6).

2. There is still sickness in the world because satan has taken advantage of our ignorance concerning our healing in Christ.

But even if our gospel is veiled, it is veiled to those who are perishing, whose minds the god of this age has blinded, who do not believe, lest the light of the gospel of the glory of Christ, who is the image of God, should shine on them (2 Corinthians 4:3-4).

F. How Is It Possible to Be Healed?

1. We can be healed by believing and trusting in God's word, that He will do as He promised.

Then Jesus said to the centurion, "Go your way; and as you have believed, so let it be done for you." And his servant was healed that same hour (Matthew 8:13).

And He said to her, "Daughter, be of good cheer; your faith has made you well. Go in peace" (Luke 8:48).

But when Jesus heard it, He answered him, saying, "Do not be afraid; only believe, and she will be made well" (Luke 8:50).

This man heard Paul speaking. Paul, observing him intently and seeing that he had faith to be healed, said with a loud voice, "Stand up straight on your feet!" And he leaped and walked (Acts 14:9-10).

2. We can be healed by confessing, speaking the truth.

Therefore I did not even think myself worthy to come to You. But say the word, and my servant will be healed (Luke 7:7).

For with the heart one believes unto righteousness, and with the mouth confession is made unto salvation [*sozo*: "wholeness, healing"] (Romans 10:10).

G. How May We Receive Healing?

1. We may receive healing by personal confession and prayer.

Confess your trespasses to one another, and pray for one another, that you may be healed. The effective, fervent prayer of a righteous man avails much (James 5:16).

2. We may receive healing by the laying on of hands.

And these signs will follow those who believe: In My name they will cast out demons; they will speak with new tongues; they will take up serpents; and if they drink anything deadly, it will by no means hurt them; they will lay hands on the sick, and they will recover (Mark 16:17-18).

And Ananias went his way and entered the house; and laying his hands on him he said, "Brother Saul, the Lord Jesus, who appeared to you on the road as you came, has sent me that you may receive your sight and be filled with the Holy Spirit" (Acts 9:17).

3. We may receive healing by the prayer of the elders.

Is anyone among you sick? Let him call for the elders of the church, and let them pray over him, anointing him with oil in the name of the Lord. And the prayer of faith will save the sick, and the Lord will raise him up. And if he has committed sins, he will be forgiven (James 5:14-15).

4. We may receive healing in the presence of the Lord in worship and praise.

You are my hiding place; You shall preserve me from trouble; You shall surround me with songs of deliverance. Selah (Psalm 32:7).

And so it was, whenever the spirit from God was upon Saul, that David would take a harp and play it with his hand. Then Saul would become refreshed and well, and the distressing spirit would depart from him (1 Samuel 16:23).

H. What May Prevent Our Healing?

1. Healing may be prevented by unbelief.

Now He could do no mighty work there, except that He laid His hands on a few sick people and healed them. And He marveled because of their unbelief.

Then He went about the villages in a circuit, teaching (Mark 6:5-6).

2. Healing may be prevented by unconfessed sins.

If I regard iniquity in my heart, the Lord will not hear (Psalm 66:18).

The Lord is far from the wicked, but He hears the prayer of the righteous (Proverbs 15:29).

But your iniquities have separated you from your God; and your sins have hidden His face from you, so that He will not hear (Isaiah 59:2).

3. Healing may be prevented by bitterness we hold against another.

But if you do not forgive men their trespasses, neither will your Father forgive your trespasses (Matthew 6:15).

The merciful man does good for his own soul, but he who is cruel troubles his own flesh (Proverbs 11:17).

I. Why May Healing Be Delayed?

1. Healing may be delayed to teach us patience and understanding of God.

And not only that, but we also glory in tribulations, knowing that tribulation produces perseverance; and perseverance, character; and character, hope (Romans 5:3-4).

My brethren, count it all joy when you fall into various trials, knowing that the testing of your faith produces patience (James 1:2-3).

2. Healing may be delayed in order to fulfill God's purpose.

Therefore let those who suffer according to the will of God commit their souls to Him in doing good, as to a faithful Creator (1 Peter 4:19).

But may the God of all grace, who called us to His eternal glory by Christ Jesus, after you have suffered a while, perfect, establish, strengthen, and settle you (1 Peter 5:10).

And He said to me, "My grace is sufficient for you, for My strength is made perfect in weakness." Therefore most gladly I will rather boast in my infirmities, that the power of Christ may rest upon me (2 Corinthians 12:9).

Let's Review What We Have Learned About the Servant of God.

1. Sickness entered the world when Adam ________________ against God.

2. ______________ uses sickness and disease to ______________ man whom God loves.

3. The curse of the Law was the ______________________ of ________________ to God's Law.

4. Jesus took all the _____________ of sin upon Himself, which includes ____________ and _______________.

5. List two ways that we may receive healing.

____

____

6. List two things that prevent healing.

____

____

Dig a Little Deeper; Grow a Little Closer

1. Read the verses below and respond to the questions that follow.

> *And He said to me, "My grace is sufficient for you, for My strength is made perfect in weakness." Therefore most gladly I will rather boast in my infirmities, that the power of Christ may rest upon me* (2 Corinthians 12:9).

2. It seems impossible that Paul, who wrote much of the New Testament, would not receive immediate healing for his sickness. What was Paul's attitude toward his infirmities?

____

____

____

3. When did the power of God rest upon Paul in this verse?

____

____

____

4. Do you think it takes more faith to trust God when we are healed or when we are not healed? Why?

____

____

____

Review Notes

Be sure to enter into the journal in this book how God responds to what you have prayed.

Books in the *Laying the FOUNDATION* Series:

Book 1—The Nature of God

- **I. The Nature of God**
- **II. The Bible**
- **III. The Creation**

Book 2—The Nature of Man

- **I. The Nature of Man**
- **II. The Fall of Man**
- **III. The Seed of Rebellion Continues**

Book 3—A Call to Faith and Obedience

- **I. Abraham: The Father of Faith and Obedience**
- **II. Israel: Called to Be the People of God**

Book 4—From Covenant to Kingdom

- **I. Taking Possession of the Promises of God**
- **II. Establishing the Kingdom**
- **III. The Message of the Prophets**
- **IV. Restoring the Remnant of Israel**

Book 5—The New Covenant

- **I. The New Covenant**
- **II. The Person of Jesus Christ**
- **III. The Nature of Jesus Christ**
- **IV. The Humiliation of Jesus Christ**

Book 6—Jesus Christ, Servant of God

I. **Wounded for Our Transgressions**

II. **Bruised for Our Iniquities**

III. **Chastised for Our Peace**

IV. **Scourged for Our Healing**

Book 7—The Exaltation of Christ

I. **The Exaltation of Jesus Christ**

II. **Jesus and the Kingdom of God**

Summary

More Titles

by Dr. Mark Hanby

YOU HAVE NOT MANY FATHERS

"My son, give me your heart." So says the proverb, echoing the heart and passion of our Father in heaven. God has spiritual "dads" all over the world whom He has filled with wisdom, knowledge, compassion, and most of all, love for those young in the faith. You do not have to go through your life untrained and unloved; uncared for and forgotten. There are fathers in Christ who are waiting to pour all they have into your heart, as Elijah did for Elisha. "My son, give me your heart."
ISBN 1-56043-166-0

YOU HAVE NOT MANY FATHERS STUDY GUIDE

ISBN 0-7684-2036-9

THE HOUSE THAT GOD BUILT

Beyond whatever man can desire is a God-given pattern for the life of the Church. Here Dr. Hanby unfolds practical applications from the design of the Tabernacle that allow us to become the house God is building today.
ISBN 1-56043-091-5

THE HOUSE THAT GOD BUILT STUDY GUIDE

ISBN 0-7684-2048-2

THE RENEWING OF THE HOLY GHOST

Do you need renewal? Everything in the natural, from birds to blood cells, must either undergo a process of renewal or enter into death. Our spiritual life is no different. With this book, your renewal can begin today!
ISBN 1-56043-031-1

ANOINTING THE UNSANCTIFIED

The anointing is more than a talented performance or an emotional response. In this book, Dr. Hanby details the essential ingredients of directional relationship that allow the Spirit of God to flow down upon the Body of Christ—and from us to the needs of a dying world.
ISBN 1-56043-071-0

PERCEIVING THE WHEEL OF GOD

On the potter's wheel, a lump of clay yields to a necessary process of careful pressure and constant twisting. Similarly, the form of true faith is shaped by a trusting response to God in a suffering situation. This book offers essential understanding for victory through the struggles of life.
ISBN 1-56043-109-1

Available at your local Christian bookstore.

For more information and sample chapters, visit www.destinyimage.com